Lingering Echoes

—————————— Collected Poems ——————————

Stania J. Slahor

iUniverse, Inc.
New York Bloomington

Lingering Echoes
Collected Poems

iUniverse books may be ordered through booksellers or by contacting:

iUniverse
1663 Liberty Drive
Bloomington, IN 47403
www.iuniverse.com
1-800-Authors (1-800-288-4677)

ISBN: 978-1-4401-6778-2 (pbk)
ISBN: 978-1-4401-6780-5 (cloth)
ISBN: 978-1-4401-6779-9 (ebook)

Printed in the United States of America

iUniverse rev. date: 10/6/09

To our wonderful planet Earth,
the innermost seat of feelings and emotions
inhabited by creative souls

Contents

Part III   joy of recognition

Forward

I think that the biggest privilege we have in the universe is language. We say: tree, sun, river, book, wind, house, cloud.... and we have a poem. A life without poetic images would be only half a life.

I was born at the beginning of the first world crisis, and spent my youth in war torn Czechoslovakia. During the twenty years following WW2, I struggled to survive under Communism and rigid state control. But the more I struggled, the more I yearned to find at least a speck of beauty, and kneel to it, and kiss it.

It's known, that suffering nations love poetry a great deal. They love to read, to recite, interpret and share its spirit-lifting ideas and feelings. My Czech countrymen have always held their poets in high esteem.

As children, we began to recite poetry by heart, as soon as we could talk. My first books were inspired by nature, animals and vividly imaginative characters, written in rhymes and beautifully illustrated by famous artists. They made a lasting impression on my soul, and influenced my decision to become an artist and poet later in life.

The first poem I wrote was published in a popular children's magazine when I was only seven, and further fuelled my poetic aspirations. There was much beauty, and so many journeys, achievements, pleasures and love during my life. But also distressful tragedies, apprehensions, disappointments, illnesses and griefs to overcome. The events and feelings I recount in my second book of English poetry, 'Lingering

Echoes', have ebbed and flowed in the depths of my mind for many years.

I embraced life situations and experiences, embellished them with my dreams, and through my perception and interpretation of life's beauty, philosophy, family and love bound them to memory.

It is my belief that in our modern, technically advanced world, there is much need for poetry to render our souls less lonely, less abrasive and angry. When we are unhappy or suffering, poetry nourishes our souls, and helps us to meditate and pray. Its music, spirit and humour gives us inner joy. It is our friend.

My husband and I still love to paddle in the first splashing waves between the sand and sea, or lie watching the clouds dissolve in summertime.

2009   Stania J. Slahor

Acknowledgement

I wish to acknowledge the work of my editor and friend, Joan Matchett, who tenderly edited my poems, despite her declining vision. She interpreted my thoughts and sent me suggestions for interesting changes. She is an admirable human being. Her artistic talent is well recognized, as well as her empathy for people with severe afflictions or misfortune. I owe her my sincere gratitude and thanks.

I still remember my first editor, the late Dr. Leon Karel, who discovered and believed in my talent for writing. His expertise and knowledge of American history and music helped me in the translation of Miroslav Ivanov's book about Antonin Dvorak, published by the Truman University Press, in Missouri, 1995.

I am grateful to Penn Kemp, an internationally recognized sound poet, for her expert proof-reading and sensitive final editing, well in tune with my poems, "Lingering Echoes". Also for peaceful and inspiring moments in her home, a place full of impressive paintings, her published books and CDs, and the intriguing souvenirs, which her husband and she have collected from around the world.

My thanks go to esteemed flutist, Ms. Laura George from New Jersey US, for her inspiring letter referring to my first book of poems: "Responding to your beautiful, magnificent 'Mercurial Journeys', I admire your courage in expressing yourself so eloquently in your second language. My favourite poems are 'The Price Of Innocence', 'Pisces', and of course, 'Count Bassie'... your colourful description of

Bassie's rhythms.... Your artwork is intriguing. Congratulation on such a triumph - you have overcome so much adversity. To be able to soar with such spirit and joy is a great inspiration to me."

I am pleased that my poems in "Mercurial Journeys", published in 2008, opened the heart of Diane Ryan from Coles, Indigo Canada. We worked together as author and bookstore-manager and a wonderful friendship developed between us. Diane remembers: "When I met Stania I was half empty, somewhat disconnected after a death of my twin sister a year earlier. But Stania's radiant smile as she approached me drew me toward her. She held a copy of her book and as I skimmed through the poems, I thought this was a treasure chest of memories. Poem after poem expressions of her passion for life, family, and friends. Who ever read these would revisit favourite moments in their life. Perhaps building sand castles as I had." A year later, Diane's note, "Stania, your new poems are amazing", encouraged me to publish my collected poems entitled "Lingering Echoes".

I acknowledge a review for "Mercurial Journeys", sent by a reader to Barnes & Noble: "... Slahor's poems are really like mercury reaching for aerial and happy heights and plummeting to the dark depths..." Similar response came from readers in Canada, USA, and Europe. Also from my doctors, who deserve my special thanks for keeping me fit to observe and enjoy this wonderful, wonderful, beautiful world.

Without the understanding of my husband, his curiosity and intuitive response to my writing, I never could have walked so confidently on this untrodden path. I am also obliged to my family, alive and dead, who shared with me their interests, problems and fun and whose lives and love inspired my narration of their stories.

Stania J. Slahor

Editor's Note

Stania Slahor and I bonded instantly when first we met on a Yucatan beach, some ten years ago. Over the years, I have become part of her extended family and an admirer of her art and poetry.

She is a woman of great talent, stamina and determination succeeding in her pursuits despite family tragedy and debilitating illness.

This book of poems is a tribute to her loves and life, an autobiography full of joys and sorrows that journeys beyond the stars.

Joan Matchett

I

---

listening to silence

motto:

"Nobody would remember you
if you keep your thoughts secret.
Force yourself to express them."
Gabriel Garcia Marquez

Jana Trnka, "Moonlight"

at the edge

my inspiring moments
exist at the edge
between the sandy beach
and the first wave
licking my feet

i grasp a lustrous shell
listen to distant echoes
from its inward ocean
and pursue
the shallow traces
of a former presence
before they sift
and wash away
the past

i do not fear death
death is only time
gone-by
set at liberty
on the opposite side

the waves
surfing waves
splashing and lapping
lustily
at my legs

everything
is just beginning –
the divine beauty
of shining pebbles
and petrified corals
veiled with floating seaweed
reaches to a climax
in the illusory fancy
lingering in man

*   *   *

sailing in moonlight

waves and waves
a labyrinth of waves
as intricate
as a network of arteries
pulsing on the surface
of the sea

white caps
shining through the dark
mark a glittering pathway
in the illuminated footsteps
of the moon

full moon
walking slowly
on the deep waters
lapping below my cabin window
our boat sailing and rocking
under the noble
southern sky

group of dolphins
bewitched and hypnotized
jump and frolic
with a school of flying fish
their bodies sleek
and phosphorescent
in the rays
of earth's unique
enamoured companion

i begin to imagine
why the mythical voyager
odysseus
beguiled by the fatal allure
of mesmerizing sirens
ordered his men
to plug their ears
with wax
and tie him to the mast
to prevent a shipwreck

*   *   *

tree-rings

tied by the cords
our ancestors attached
to ancient trees
we keep accurate records
of every event
logged in the core
of our brain

our memory
is a chronicle
exact and true to life
mapped like the wooden rings
under the bark
of full-grown trees
disclosing the past

decoded
our concealed secrets
– sometimes grave-dark
that we hide
even from people
in our confidence –
reveal the changes
in private climate
with their impact
upon the nature
of the human race

enduring labour
of ebbs and flows
the unrestrained anger
of murdering storms
our moonstruck moods
spin from high noon
to the deepest dark

all the same
every experience –
some beyond reason
and understanding –
will number our days
whether we seek to forget
or not

*   *   *

mutilated

five minutes
from a street car stop
to my hilltop home
a throng of sycamore trees
whispered to me in the dark
warning

tomorrow we die
they said
they'll bring their saws and axes
lop our branches at the shoulders
leave us naked
on the sidewalk
bleeding sap

they must be wrong
i thought

noble and free
and beautiful they were
the only embellishment
of this ugly street

it cannot be done

but they came
a whole army of men
ready to kill
mutilate and rape
consumed with disdain
lopping and chopping
impersonal

in the morning
on my way from home
i had to pass
among the naked trunks
standing tall and bare
yet still firm
and proud

the desecrated cemetery
of dismembered monuments
marked by a tiny drop
of enduring hope
for another spring

*　　*　　*

memory

memory has wings
sits quietly on my shoulder
listens to whispers
picks up small bits
of my heart

conceived in the nest
of my mind
she is feathered
with vivid images
sharp opinions
and judgments
gathered from the past

suddenly
she takes wing
to an unseen distant garden
carrying away my nightmares
the enduring losses
in life

every once in a while
she flies back
and i feed her again
till my heart
is spent
and cannot remember
hurt anymore

*   *   *

phi - divine pattern

the desire
to discover
and unlock a secret
of timeless beauty
in a large complexity of world
might be
genetically programmed
in the human dna

this phenomenon
recognized as a golden ratio
is the basic rule
bonding the universe

the creative effort
of nature's workshop
the ceaseless reproduction of species
by combination of golden sections
in a whole
prevails around us
in time

the beautiful shapes
of propagative seeds
flower petals
pistils and stigmas
pagodas of pine cones
enfold the innate capability
of nature

we can see
the divine design
in every drop of water
transformed
to intricate patterns of snowflakes
bird wings
aeroplanes
drifting desert dunes
or ocean waves

the golden ratio
implanted in human minds
pulses in music
art and drama
in mathematics
enigmatic structures
of egyptian pyramids
greek temples
michelangelo's sistine chapel
astonishing
the civilized world

everlasting miracle
the golden sections
cast the die
for divine beauty
and harmony
in the mona lisa's
mysterious smile
the fabulous sculpture
of queen nefertiti
marilyn monroe's
alluring features and charm

and store all
in human memory
as intensely desirable
to the eye

*　　*　　*

Jana Trnka, "Clouds"

dissolving clouds

we embraced
we kissed
and laughed
but until you boasted
that you could dissolve a cloud
i didn't know
how much i loved you

remember the summer day
we made love
in a lonely clearing
and tired and sated
lay in the crumpled grass
counting white sheep
grazing blue meadows
in the sky

you taught me
to direct my mind
toward a cloud
a puff of cotton
and to separate and dissolve
one fluffy sheep
from the peaceful
celestial herd

in a couple of minutes
the rounded cloudlet
began to vapour and swirl
and suddenly vanished
without a trace
from our sight

ever since
you have been my magician
wielding great power
over my dreams
and heart

*   *   *

sleeping in a meadow

now
we have a new king-size bed
a fragrant blooming meadow
fenced by an arched headboard
artfully turned
on the craftsman's lathe

we breath in gallons
of fresh unpolluted air
free from dust mites
old quarrels
farts and aches
and every night
on a kite
fly above the city
holding hands

we bought
two single mattresses
our reverie riverbanks
where every night
we go to fish
for our private moons
and independent dreams

like depleted batteries
we recharge overnight
with vital energy

and wake up
in the morning
satisfied

*   *   *

snowman

you are a snowman
unresponsive
and cold
made of icy snowballs
squashed into layers
of your silent wishes
and unpredictable moods

yet after a snowstorm
i'll be your sun
playfully kissing
and melting
your lovelorn body
resurrected
from icy quiescence
by my charm

*   *   *

never patch love

we can fix everything
but a broken heart!

announced the old sign
hanging in front
of uncle's welding store
in our town

in fact
people can patch
repair
fix
and restore
all material articles
or mechanical devices
most severely impaired things

they can perform bypasses
restart hearts
but they never
never can resurrect love

since love is
as delicate and fragile
as fine porcelain
precious as crystal
we must tenderly finger
caress and hold her
with both our hands and heart

*   *   *

snake-man

i better not ask you
what you have brought
in a wicker basket
thrown in anger
on our kitchen floor

weird and tattered
it spills open
and a twisted tangle
of poisonous snakes
escapes and threatens
to bite me
if i utter
a word

*   *   *

don't sear my heart

you are the sun
of many unknown faces
emitting light
in mercurial moods

i tried
to catch you
trick you into a net
but the flamboyant butterfly
became a flame
branding his name
into my sensitive skin

don't sear my heart
i watch you
through sunglasses
firing swift bullets
from a blazing gun

you bronze me lovingly
but cannot control
your unrestrained passion
and lust

heedless i dive
under the parasol
and lie
contentedly waiting
for a rose sunset
in your amorous arms

*   *   *

fisherman

a passionate fisherman
under a stone bridge
in burleigh falls
speaking birdy
with a blue heron
quacking and blabbing
trumpet-beak syllables
which i don't understand
feeling so lonely
forever trapped
in the seine fishing net
of his hollow heart

*   *   *

Jana Trnka, "Golden Rays"

phenomenon

gliding silently
beneath the waves
thousands of golden rays
gilded the vast rolling waters
of the gulf of mexico
as they migrated
from western florida
to the yucatan coast

safe from the rays'
poisonous stingers
as we floated unharmed
in our sailboat
surrounded
by frolicking schools
we experienced
magnificent nature
at its best

extending over the surface
in a great variety
of warm golden shades
the beautiful rays
moved peacefully
and gently
like giant autumn leaves
floating on a leisurely wind

the unforgettable hours
spent in close observation
deeply affected
our innermost feelings
about the nature's
unending carnival

*   *   *

hummingbird

a tiny winged bullet
buzzing oscillator
and incurable drunkard
the hummingbird

intoxicated
by beauty of the nature
addicted to nectar
it flutters
and flashes
in and out
romantically attracted
by the colour red

high spirited
and weightless
it jets
from flower to flower
courting vines
festooned with sweet
hanging blossoms
the golden flutes
and clarinets

*   *   *

heartwood

my head
is stubborn
and unyielding
like an old cutting board
from my kitchen keepsakes
iron-hard

cut from an oak
durable and strong
its hand-planed surface
resists the force of hardship
without a scar

its heartwood core
grown denser
and denser
over an infinitely long time
keeps the trunk
from defeat
and yielding
to violent squalls

as the tree matures
deposits of wastes
clog its vessels
with resins
tannin
gums
and essential oils
embracing the air
with the sweet perfume
of life

like a centennial oak
with the weather-beaten crown
i am the obstinate
hard-minded woman –
my thirsty roots
implanted deeply
search for the hidden wells
in motherly soil

*　　*　　*

deafness

my deafness
a different way to listen
in small increments
as i age

it is my gift
to block unpleasant sounds
mind-polluting noises
and interferences
with the keen perception
of inward hearing

happy and content
(allegedly withdrawn)
within my reduced range
i love to listen
to silence

silence
as heavy as the clouds
almost too high
for rain

sounds
lowered and elevated in pitch
that become inaudible
to my ears

of necessity
i learned to hear
the quiet wings of butterflies
alighting gently
on my feet

*   *   *

one way journey

a delicate cataract surgery
set me on a journey
through the dark tunnel
in my brain

after the quick removal
of a cloudy lens in the impaired eye
the fleeting streams
of sparkling meteors
entered my inner sight
and deleted ghost spots
that had invaded
my visual field
with the glares and halos
for a decade

my one-way journey
reminded me
of overnight travel
on a steam-engine express train

the burning smoke
like the fiery tail of a comet
spit from the iron chimney
and illuminated a pane
of my compartment's
pitch-dark window
with the rocketing speed
of fireworks

the expert implant
of an artificial intra-ocular lens
brightened the inner sky
of my brain,
and restored
the view
of the shapes and colours
i missed so badly

*   *   *

acupuncture

my naked body feels
like a fallow field
waiting to be ploughed
and planted
with fine
acupuncture needles
expertly inserted
at specific points
by a soft-handed
chinese doctor

a replica
of claude monet's landscape
scrawled by a curious
morning sunbeam
peeping through chinks
of psychedelic blinds
and lingering on lilacs
in an old china-bowl
on the window ledge

traditional
soft chinese music
induces me to meditate

the chi
a driving force of life
flows through the network
of intricate pathways
identified and mapped
by the chinese
centuries ago

after the treatment
i feel like a gauzy cloud
pinned to the sky
by afternoon sun
in the late bloom

featherweight
and free of painful tension
i sense a flow of bubbling streams
restoring me
to harmonious health

*   *   *

funeral of a young girl

they attended her funeral
murmuring
we should sue the hospital
doctors
and nurses
for malpractice

one million dollars at least
they said
for such great grief
and pain

still
after four decades
i keep my daughter's indigo shawl
and if i close my eyes
can smell
her shiny umber hair
and see it flutter
in the wind
on her way home

her little tote with a comb
hairpins and lipstick
dried out pen
student's card
and dim mirror
that preserves the likeness
of her lovely face

everything still touchable
and kissable
no money can buy

*　　*　　*

flowerbeds

after my escape
with a sole suitcase
and a frightened teenage daughter
i braved
exhausting proceedings
of divorce
gossipy neighbours's contempt
daring to recover
my lost dreams
and past

together
we set up
two unusual flowerbeds
as lively symbols
of our mutual love
and longing
for a new life

inspired by the little mermaid
in andersen's
under-the-sea fairy tale
my daughter planted
a circular bed
with yellow marigolds
fluttering joyfully
like a dancing sun

i grew the scores
of showy rudbeckias
in the shape
of five-armed starfish
thrusting
and waving
their red gleaming petals
ready to revive
my lonely heart

*   *   *

gift

the stainless steel cutlery
our daughter gave us
for our first christmas
in canada
began now to tarnish
and corrode
in our kitchen drawer

working
in a small restaurant
as a waitress
she paid for the precious gift
from her tips
saved for the university courses
she wanted to attend
the next year

three decades have passed
since she died
yet
using the knives
forks and spoons
from the old set
and listening to the clear clinks
of their heartbeats
brings us back
her untarnished love

*   *   *

II

---

visits with beauty

motto:

"Each object is in reality
a small virtual volcano."
Helene Cixous

motto:

"Love, like death, changes everything"
Gabriel Garcia Marquez

Jana Trnka, "April"

april ploughing

on the bohemian upland
farmer vaclav pleva
was to plough
his small clay tract
of fallow field

at high noon
under the blue april sky
he harnessed his powerful ox
and set to work

heel!
the farmer commanded
holding the reins firmly
but the stubborn animal
wasn't in the mood
for orders

the old man in a frenzy
beseeched and whipped
the obstinate ox
but the animal's muzzle
steaming with foam
gave him the discouraging warning
of imminent risk

young and full of fantasies
i approached
grabbed the halter
and as the animal's anger quickly abated
i led him gently
to plough the initial furrow

all of a sudden
i felt far-away and dauntless
performing the acrobatic feats
of bull vaulting
and frivolous somersaults
for a great pleasure
of the king minos

strong enough
to handle
the fire breathing minotaur
threatening to trample poor vaclav
under his feet
i proudly transformed
the fearsome ox
into an obedient
beast of burden

* * *

fields

why did we travel
that unpaved road
to see the bygone farm
we sold once
for petty gain?

the depleted fields
we had tilled and planted
with acres of corn
soya beans
winter wheat
and hope

until our hands
became gnarled
callused branches
and bloodthirsty creditors
began to gorge
from rooftop
to empty cellar
on our insolvent homestead

*   *   *

geologist

on the research trip
along the donau river
the geologist laco molnar
was lost from your team
for several troubled hours

when you found him
in the full-moon night
he stood naked
knee-high
in a narrow tributary
playfully washing
the laughing gypsy-girl
he brought to camp
for a night

geologists
have well-trained eyes
for the voluptuous lines
of surveyed landscapes
the buxom vistas
and alluring slopes
of lovely curved hips
and elevated breasts

how exciting
to be the winsome territory
my horse-hoofed centaur
travels and explores
with love

*   *   *

erratic boulder

there was a mammoth
sleeping by the route
to our pasture
on the farm

an enormous boulder
pushed ruthlessly
along by the force
of the north-american icecap
at the end
of the ice age

tumbled
over the frozen ground
finally unfastened
from the icy grip
it lay now free
basking
his ancient skin
in the warm sun

i loved to visit
this marvellous creature
listening anxiously
to his thousand muted pipes
vibrant and trilling
at my touch

one by one
i tried to decode
the weighty messages
that warned
of imminent danger
beaming so gently
from his rocky heart

*   *   *

country mass

the lofty cathedral
a silver-weathered
centenarian barn
surrounded by a ring
of ripening wheat
psalm-green pastures
and random bowing
apple trees

inside the spacious lodge
a fragrance of fresh-cut hay
enhanced gently
my senses

humbled i lifted my arms
and let my spirit wing
up to the rustic rafters
dotted with nests
of darting swallows

open crevices
between the weather-beaten
cedar planks
allowed the sun's rays
to warm and penetrate
this sacred place
with shimmering sheets
of brilliant light
creating a solemn atmosphere
for the celebration
of a country mass

*   *   *

pastoral prelude

classic organ music
broadcast on the radio
reminded me
of an old chapel
under mountain slopes

in the nave
a full-bearded sexton
inflated the bellows
of the huge antique organ
and revived
the wheezing
artfully carved pipes

the organist's improvisations
of bach's pastoral prelude
aroused the spirit
intensified by the fresh
mountain air

after a tacit pause
the priest
yielded to the choir
and my mother's
resounding voice
soared to the vaulted ceiling
filling the entire space
and fast pulsing hearts
with joy

my mother passed away
years ago
but my memory
of the pastoral mass
ever so often
brings her back to me
in her prime

*   *   *

rain

a young girl
on a paved sidewalk
listens to the raindrops
drumming her umbrella
as she straddles
a large puddle
and laughs

she jumps and stamps
as muddy silky water
spatters and splashes
her pumps

drop drop drop
lush singing rain
falls on a window-pane
girl's cheeks
umbrella
withering flowers
a wonderful
wonderful
r
    a
       i
         n

*   *   *

life's everywhere

if life is electricity
the entire earth
has to be
alive

you
i
trees
rocks
bodies of oceans
the ever-changing sky
bolting down lightning
with roaring
thunderclaps

no matter
how far we go
we always find life

eagerly
we touch a star
with competing desire
to explore
and discover
who we really are

*   *   *

Jana Trnka, " Stars"

where
have all those bright stars gone?

we love our cities
dotted by phosphorescent neon streetlights
the red and yellow ribbons
of rushing vehicles
magically embellishing
the night

highlighted playgrounds
and utopian airports
sky-rising towers
striving for brightness
against the huge glittering stars

we moved to a suburbs
and seduced
by the beauty of the starry sky
beneath our hillside home
we suddenly took notice
of the gradual invasion
of the boldly beaming city
drawing ever so near

only a decade later
the city lights
brighter and brighter
flood the valley
extinguish the stars

in his hawk tower poems
the american poet
robinson jeffers
lamented the artless drift
of civilization
rapidly approaching
his secluded
pacific coast home

i recall his voice
as i mourn
our diamond-studded nights
gradually slipping away
from the sky

*   *   *

kaleidoscope

a play of colours
lines
figures and sparks
whirlpools of puzzles
reflected
in the magic looking-glass
of a kaleidoscopic tube

the upside-down world
of diametrical opposites
antithesis
antimatter
antimissiles
antipodes
in the global shift

a to and fro
mirage
ice-crystals glowing
in rainbow vision
under a mock sun

an iridescent sky
shooting stars
breaking news
vital messages
transmitted out of solar system
and time

expanding universe
doodle constellations
zodiac signs
foretell destiny
relations and love

galileo's disciple
stephen hawking
gigantic observatories
with sophisticated telescopes
gaze toward vast nebulae
veiled in haze

*   *   *

eclipse

the end of the world

the debuting actor
furtively tiptoes
over the grand stage
of the yucatan sky

full-moon
hypnotizing and bright
meets face to face
with valiant earth
in darkening space

in the next act
its illuminated surface
grows gruesomely pale
and ghostly red
under the shade
of earth's global scope
blocking the sun's
travelling rays

stunned by the phenomenon
the agitated spectators
fearfully anticipate
that the world might collapse
and end

ultimately
when the eclipse culminates
stars begin to sparkle
glisten again
and the dark curtain opens
upon the unmasked face
of the full moon

*   *   *

dark river to antares

on astronomy picture of the day

there is a giant star
— antares —
embedded in the lush meadows
of a colourful nebula
rho ophiuchi

its brilliant
unrestrained light
recalls the intricate strands
of human longing

from the blue womb
of a distant nebula
a slow murky cloud
of dark river
oozes mischievously
toward antares's
radiating heart

without hesitation
it creeps slowly
along the incessant
meandering route
severely testing
kind spirit
of universe

its ominous floating dust
greedily absorbs the flickering light
of background stars
into its trap

like death
swathed in a thick veil
it guilefully conceals
the past's catastrophic events
surrounding the site

still
as an ambitious
high-tech-society
we seek to reach beyond
the prevailing antares
up to unknown territories
and to discover
how far freedom and truth can go
in time and space

*   *   *

above lake erie

a lively dream
took me for a flight
over the iridescent firmament
beyond lake erie

feeling free
and circling high
on wings of seagulls
i dove into clouds

waves of dizziness
exaggerated by images
of the deep waters
billowing beneath

"what am i doing here?
it's dangerous"
i whispered in awe

but suddenly
a strong masculine hand
reached for my arm
and holding me safely
joined me in my flight

the glittering surface
of the lake far bellow
looked like a giant map
guiding me where?

the mysterious hand
on my arm
lessened my fears
and i was able to follow
the telepathic messages
from the invisible navigator

after a short flight
he pointed out
the path of a narrow creek
on the opposite american coast
as if to identify
a significant place

next morning
a long-distance call
announced the disappearance
of our friend
during his solitary fishing trip
in a small motor boat
along the canadian
wilderness shore

several days later
his corpse was found
near the creek estuary
which i had previously seen
on the mental map
in my dream

*   *   *

hurricane

a threatening wave
a hundred feet high
towered upon the ferocious ocean
bore down
on the abandoned long island beaches
a marauding beast
looking for prey

unaware of the danger
the four of us held hands
stood firm together
against the buffering wind
as a thick layer
of repulsive yellow foam
whisked and churned
in the devil's caldron
of the raging sea
began inundating
the coast

a howling squall
forced us to retreat
from the shore
to our plundered host-town
littered with broken branches
uprooted trees
shattered windows
and blown away roofs

stunned
we finally realized
we too could have been
just as easily uprooted
but for sheer luck

*   *   *

beethoven
on the top of the mountain

finding a concert piano
on the very top
of rysy mountain
in the spectacular high tatras
seemed to be a joke
until the lanky ageless man
dressed in black
appeared at the very end
of a narrow
boulder strewn path

fascinated
we watched
as he leaned
over the instrument
and began to play

beethoven's piano concerto #4
resounded from the cracked
yellowing keyboard
and majestic music
pushed apart
the thick drizzling fog
smothering the peaks

lingering clouds underfoot
receded quickly
and opened a vista
of sky-touching ridges
chasms and gorges

crisscrossed with delicate webs
of animal trails
gushing cascades
and bottomless emerald tarns

but after a short movement
the concert abruptly ended
on a high vibrant beat
and behind our backs
with the last echo
of his inspiring performance
the mysterious musician disappeared

*   *   *

Jana Trnka, "Overboard"

roses overboard

wrecked
we were wrecked
our propeller broken
when we hit
a sunken stone wall
a good distance
from the lake huron coast

from the lighthouse
its crew signalled us
to wait

following boccaccio's decameron
we told our life-stories
funny
scandalous or sad
while eating
last handfuls of plums

suddenly
a rumble of thunder
announced a storm
approaching over the paling lake

the dark fearsome front
raced menacingly
across the sky
and a furious wind
strong and wild
turned the placid lake
into the most perilous of waters
and set the metre-high waves
to lifting and rocking
our featherweight boat

in the dark
a faint blinking light
headed toward our helpless wreck
lurching and plunging
behind each towering wave

finally
two brave coast guards
threw us a cable
hooked us to their sturdy boat
and the most frightening passage
of my life began

terrified
i gripped the cold railing
and stared into the fathomless depths
as looming mountains
of dark-green water
tossed our guardian vessel about
like a toy

what majesty
what mighty power
we had to overcome!

i became sick
vomiting roses
beautiful red roses
thrown into the lake's trapdoor
overboard
for all men drowned
in the abysmal peril
of that night

"were you scared?"
our angel-guardian asked me
as i stood
startled and pale
on the harbour shore

"no!"
i denied his notion
"it was fun"

"no?
well, we were"
he laughed

*   *   *

sailing with monarchs

after a ghastly midnight storm
lake erie lay flat
in the morning sun
and waiting
for the first breath of wind
to lift and billow
the languorous sails
we sat motionless
within sight of shore

a long hour of boring idleness
turned our dream
of dancing on the bright horizon
with a team
of coquetting yachts
to ashes

with a small needle
and thread from my purse
i began patching a few holes
in the stiffening canvas
of tattered sails
while a large swarm
of migrating monarchs
seeking an oasis
after their long
exhausting flight over the lake
alighted softly on the boat

in a flash
our hair
sails
and cracking vessel
were covered
with a fine lace
fabricated of their wings

*   *   *

repatriation

an abandoned
sudetenland farmstead
surrounded
by an overgrown garden
of thorny roses
halting trespassers
tempted me
to explore

i forced open
the heavy rustic door
to evil-smelling air
hung in the dark wet corridor
leading to musty country kitchen
occupied generations back
by german farmers

a sad picture
of a household
left behind vandalized
by covetous interlopers

or
was it an act of reprisal?

on the huge mildewed table
lay a pair of broken bowls
deformed tablespoons
while a long kitchen knife
perhaps tossed in anger
lay on the dusty floor

between the pictures
of favourite saints
hung a heavy cross
with the crucified christ
to whom
nobody prays
anymore

in the attic
a bundle of children's worn-out clothes
locally-made wooden toys
burdened my heart
with sudden grief

oh politics!
how could it divide people
nations
the whole world

saddened i opened
an old wooden chest
and found
several family photographs
overlooked during the ransack

surprise!
on the bottom
lay a decoration
of the fascist army
a ww2 distinguished cross
and a portrait
of an arrogant ss officer
bearing the farmer's family features

remembering
a couple of my relatives
annihilated in the notorious
concentration camps
my ideas
about forced repatriation
quickly vanished

*   *   *

journey to india

looking for my son
during his sojourn in india
i googled a map
of the controversial subcontinent
on my monitor

with every click
i moved
from one mind-boggling image
to another
as tiny squares
like miniature postcards
designated
important geographical sites
of its terrain

the sacred
- yet heavily polluted -
ganges river
beloved of her people
a historic symbol
of india's ancient culture
ever changing
ever flowing
from the majestic himalayas
into bengal bay

the monumental architecture
of white-marble temples
fairy-tale palaces
fountains
and mythical statues
compelling me to continue
my search

to sightsee
in overpopulated cities
where rich and poor
live side by side
vibrant and noisy
with slow moving traffic
squeezing its way
through plugged arteries
toward their ancient hearts

to follow
honking automobiles
thwarted by overstuffed rickshaws
three-wheeled velotaxis
and teetering rack wagons
pulled by skinny
hunchback cows

to surf
through busy streets
fringed by modern housing
exotic gardens
flanked by shocking slums
and raucous sidewalk bazaars

to join
the colourful trains
of proud
sari-clad Indian women
balancing huge vessels
on their heads

to hear
worshippers say
if you mix a little phial
of the ganges' sacred water
– purported by the hindus
never to stink
or rot –
with any other source
the entire mixture
is deemed to be the holy water
of the ganges
as well

imbued with healing
and cleansing properties
that restore the spirit
and used in sacred rituals
ensures good health

what a mysterious place
to travel through!

*   *   *

boots

the echo
of marching
gestapo boots
on stony flights of stairs
in my high school
during ww2
has never faded

never been silenced

it lay waiting
upon the alumni meeting
of our revolutionary class
of 42
under the stucco
renaissance ceiling

it will always be there

the germans
suffering great losses
in russia's frozen steppes
and during the guerrilla warfare
in occupied europe
turned their hate-filled eyes
on the local resistance

they found a cell of freedom fighters
led by the teachers
senior students
and principal
right in my school

i remember
listening to the stomp of gestapo boots
interrupting classes
the entire school
expectant and scared

the terrifying sounds of opening doors
roared names
breaking the silence
and our hearts

more footsteps
dragging and bumping resisting bodies
down each flight

slamming doors on idling trucks
waiting to transport
singled out offenders
never to be seen again

arrested and imprisoned
without warrant
liquidated one by one
in nazi concentration camps

horrifying footsteps
on those stone stairs
echoing forever

*   *   *

runs / ladders

the old fashioned ww2 stockings
we used to wear to school
church and promenade
on rendezvous dates
that sometimes ended
in the nearest air-raid shelter
became my everyday pain

the fidgety seams
must always be kept straight
on the calves
a difficult task
for a girl of my age
without a mirror
at hand

the tiny run
would appear
and begin to creep
as i eased the cobweb-stockings
over my skinny teenage leg

the critical eyes
i sensed
watching it
crawl out
from the heel
of wadded shoe
over my knobby knee
under my pleated skirt
as i hurried
along the busy street

unsightly ladders
in my only pair of stockings
traded for precious ration points
or illegally purchased
on the black market
burning under the glances
of passers-by
like a fire
i couldn't ignore
or put out

* * *

III

---

joy of recognition

motto:

"I would give wings to the children,
but I would leave the child alone
so that he could learn how to fly on his own."
Gabriel Garcia Marquez

Jana Trnka, "Seed of heaven"

neek kaan

the seed of heaven

the mayas
call the blazing sun
neek kaan
the seed of heaven

they observe it
rising to its zenith in the morning
and every afternoon
falling from the sky
embedding itself
in the distant horizon
to rest and germinate
overnight

next morning
its glorious burst into fiery flower
gives to mayas good reason
to celebrate
a new day

*   *   *

bedside tables

during our first few years
in canada
we tried to pretend
to our visiting
old-country relatives
that our life in exile
was well established
at that time

still
we needed lots of courage
and imagination to devise
an adequate
and modest household

we faced the challenge
with meagre means
and fewer instincts
than nesting birds
of creating
a nice-looking household

without steady jobs
or money to buy
second-hand furniture
from charity storerooms
our humble household was far
from what we could afford

one of our ideas
was to make
fancy bedside tables
of round cardboard boxes
from the cheese factory
upholstered with remnants
of brocade curtains
to camouflage
our lack of funds

yet years later
we remembered with laughter
how well
the practical design
fit our initial life style

*   *   *

two heads - one body

a little boy
has painted a picture
representing his family
in his artless way

blessed by a lack of inhibition
the three year old
depicted his small
wonderful world
inhabited by his parents
and himself
on a red
a4 construction paper
in his unique way

it's me
he pointed out
to a tall
oversized figure
with a big stomach

beside him
stood much smaller parents
earmarked by two large heads
joined by a common
bubble-body

perhaps
our grandson
will never become an artist
but the longer i study his picture
the more
i can understand
childhood's innocent philosophy
and the secret
behind his weird image
of the world

*   *   *

four animal tales

for martin

elephant

a panting locomotive
of an elephant's powerful body
moves over the vast
african plain

with trumpet-trunk hoisted
his enormous ears
like a pair of flapping wings
take him up slowly
into the ruddy sky

flying high
and lacking skill
he pilots at random
towards a nearest
whipped cream cloud
but too heavy
and blunt
gets spat
into mud

*   *   *

rhino

clumsy noisy
angry and mad
rattle-tattle rhino
tried to shake a land

to make the earthquake
he thrust in vain
his thick ivory horn
against the rigid
village fence

thrown aside
by the violent kick-back
the furious rhino
runs quick away
like a snorting
transcontinental
train

*　　*　　*

giraffe

the tallest
of all land-living animals
a brown spotted
long-necked giraffe
moves within a large herd
on the vast plains
of the african steppe

undisturbed
by intrusive safari party
the teetering
lookout-tower
browses and munches
silky twigs and leaves
from the tops of fanning
mimosa trees

but when chased by lion
or predatory cheetah
the giraffe
bounds away
with the long strides
and loops
blown along
by dusty hot
savannah wind

*   *   *

polar bear

according
to an old inuit folktales
the bears are humans

they live
in their own houses
but for going outside
they put on a heavy bear coat
becoming violent
predatory hunters

the spirits
of bears and humans
are closely related
and often change
forth and back

wearing bear tooth
in a necklace
or sewn into a hat
gives the human heart
great talismanic power
over the realms
of nature and spirit

*　　*　　*

crisis

in memory of my parents

my mother said
when i was born
there was a crisis
and my father
a young engineer
on the state railway
lost his job
and was transferred
to do subordinate work
in a faraway city

they had no money
for a baby-coach
people went hungry to bed
and my father
who sent home
most of his meagre earnings
and kept only a little
for scarce meals
took a lonely walk
in deserted streets
counting shut doors
and windows

the crisis
we sincerely hoped
would never come back
as far as we lived

yet
eighty years later
after a long period
of growing wealth and prosperity
our security
seems to be shaken

i can envisage
walking hungry
in the streets
counting shut windows
and the barred doors

* * *

old lady's treasure

her silver hair
bursting milkweed pods
of pure silk
spindle-spun
gossamer webs
woven on the purring loom
of indian summer

the unrestrained
wavy mane
never violated by perms
or artificial dyes
a rich dowry
handed down
from her mom

unabashed
by the outdated style
she desires to age gracefully
reposing in wintertime

*   *   *

november

a cold november morning
window panes obscured
by falling leaves
and teardrops
of embittered
rain

no lights
no signs
of illegible street-names
to show me the passage
to my mother's
heart

my right to enter
seemed forever denied
by the waft of death

she died
my mother died
i suddenly knew
without being told

her flame snuffed out

the end

yet she bequeathed me
the inheritance
hoarded for me
since i left home

five sleeping beehives
to be opened
in the spring
one husky dog
to stroke
with love
and a handful
of long kept secrets
she whispers to me
in my sleep

*   *   *

secret ingredient

i always loved
to watch my mother
cooking our favourite meals

she was a great cook!
she didn't need to weigh
or measure
any of the ingredients
to create
a fantastic dish
without a recipe

she just put together
the right amounts of this
dollops of that
with pinches of spices
and fragrant herbs

later on
i discovered
the secret ingredient
for blending her wonderful dishes
of epicurean delight
with heavenly taste

her love

*   *   *

without borders

time went by
i lost my youthful wings
and became able
to fly
only in dreams

weightless
like a parachute
of dandelion seeds
i pirouette
above the vast countryside
searching broad lakes
for the lost reflections
of my youthful flights

in dreams
i dare
there are no borders
in the sky

*   *   *

About Jana Trnka

Jana Trnka, a graduate of the Academy of Visual Arts in Bratislava, Slovak Republic, an internationally acclaimed Swiss painter, sculptor and creator of several monumental paintings. She works with a huge palette of colours and techniques in sensitive intricate patterns.

Trnka's extraordinary painting, "Peace World", on the jacket, and seven images in this collection show her swinging moods within an abstract mode that reveals the infinity of her thematic compositions and her striking contemporary vision. By creating a sensation of vibration in shimmering water, light and in a vast space, she touches the very core of Slahor's poetry. As a world-wide traveller, she gives witness to the poet's emotions, desires, disappointments and hopes, bonding them in a brilliant mosaic of the heart.

Ms. Jana Trnka has lived in Lausanne, Switzerland, for 26 years.

You can see more of Jana Trnka's work by visiting her website: www.trnkajana.com